Focus on

The Great Gatsby

by F. Scott Fitzgerald

Peter Davies

Greenwich Exchange, London

Focus on
The Great Gatsby
©Peter Davies 2008

First published in Great Britain in 2008
All rights reserved

Printed and bound by Q3 Digital/Litho, Loughborough
Tel: 01509 213456
Typesetting and layout by Jude Keen, London
Tel: 020 8355 4541
Cover design by December Publications, Belfast
Tel: 028 90286559

Greenwich Exchange Website: www.greenex.co.uk

Cataloguing in Publication Data is available from the
British Library

ISBN-13: 978-1-906075-29-3

To Libby

Contents

1

Gatsby and the American Dream

In the autumn of 1924, while still working on a revision of his third novel, which ultimately appeared in April the following year as *The Great Gatsby*, Scott Fitzgerald was excitedly telling Maxwell Perkins, his editor at Scribner's, that his new book "is about the best American novel ever written", and his New York agent Harold Ober, that it is "head and shoulders over everything I've done". In his two previous novels, *This Side of Paradise* (1920) and *The Beautiful and Damned* (1922) besides a host of short stories in some of the US's most influential periodicals, Fitzgerald had already established himself as a precocious commentator on the social "state of the nation" in America. The titles of his two popular short story collections to that date, *Flappers and Philosophers* (1920) and *Tales of the Jazz Age* (1922), speak for themselves. They had established Fitzgerald as an author whose perceptions were absolutely on the pulse of contemporary America, and the very large sales of his work meant that his reputation went far beyond the relatively small number of discerning critics. To his wide readership his work appeared to be creating a mental and moral vocabulary in which an entire generation could view itself. His output was that happy combination of 'literary' and bestselling, so he could regard himself purely and simply as a professional writer from an early age.

Between the popular success of *This Side of Paradise* and the short stories, and the composition of *The Great Gatsby*, there was to be a sea change in Fitzgerald's thinking about what fiction should be. His early admiration for American realists like Frank Norris and Theodore Dreiser and for such

British figures as H.G. Wells and Compton Mackenzie, who had been in vogue when he was at Princeton, was gradually replaced by a consciousness that the way 'forward' in the novel was being dictated by those authors to whose outlook an awareness of the vital importance of technique was germane. Notable among these of course had been Henry James, but it was Joseph Conrad, who was to die in 1924 while *Gatsby* was being written, who was the most obviously persuasive influence. In his preface to *The Nigger of the Narcissus* Conrad had set forth with crystal clarity in its opening line what serious fiction should be: "A work that aspires, however humbly, to the condition of art should carry its justification in every line." Fitzgerald took this dictum absolutely to himself. His new novel would be something very different from the spontaneous, youthful outpourings of *This Side of Paradise*. It should not be a "loose, baggy monster", as James had stigmatised the large European novels of the 19th century. Gatsby is a meticulously *planned* novel and we are constantly aware of it as being a thing of hardworking sentences.

Fitzgerald was emboldened by Conrad's dictum, "My task which I am trying to achieve is, by the power of the written word to make you hear, to make you feel – it is, before all, to make you see," to progress beyond his early success to a new and high seriousness of purpose. The verdict on Gatsby, which we are given at the beginning, not the end, of the story as if to lay down a marker for the level of the novel's concerns, is quintessentially Conradian: "No – Gatsby turned out all right at the end; it is what preyed on Gatsby, what foul dust floated in the wake of his dreams that temporarily closed out my interest in the abortive sorrows and shortwinded elations of men." It demands that we do not shirk rigorous engagement with the moral complexity of what is to follow.

Paradoxically, in view of the reputation and sales it has achieved since Fitzgerald's death in 1940 at the age of only 44, *The Great Gatsby* did not, in the years immediately following its publication, become a popular success. True, it was greatly admired by a number of his contemporary writers, notable

2

among them T.S. Eliot, who told Fitzgerald in a letter that it was "the first step that American fiction has taken since Henry James". Gertrude Stein, Edith Wharton, and the slightly younger Ernest Hemingway, himself at that time at the outset of his career as an author, were also warm in their approval. But neither this admiration, however widely circulated among writers, nor the wholehearted support for the novel from Perkins at Scribner's was enough to help Fitzgerald out of the financial abyss into which his extravagant social life with his beautiful but unstable Jazz-Age wife, Zelda, had plunged him.

His premature death was to change all this with remarkable speed. If *This Side of Paradise* had had a certain revelatory value in its lifting of the lid off the sexual mores of the middle-class American adolescent of the period, and *The Beautiful and Damned* had, with all its faults, administered something of a shock to the system with the jaded eye it cast, in particular, on the corrosive effect of marriage, *The Great Gatsby* was soon being hailed as being nothing less than a paradigm of America itself, a remarkable multifaceted construct of reality and myth. Its eponymous protagonist and his aspirations were seen to be an embodiment of the American Dream. To the less savoury aspects of this dream, however, Fitzgerald was regarded as administering an unsparing examination, questioning the validity of such of its inviolable components as personal freedom and prosperity, when compared with loyalty to friendship and personal kindness – especially to those less fortunate than oneself.

The American Dream had been variously defined by that country's writers and thinkers as being either a matter of personal freedom and the germination of the potential within the individual to achieve success – political, financial, entrepreneurial, industrial – that the notion carried with it, or as a matter of the national psyche, the qualities of sturdy individualism combined, especially at times of crisis, with the capacity for the exercise of collective will that had created the unique character of the nation from the late 17th century onwards.

Fitzgerald was later, at the end of his short story *The Swimmers* (1929), to attempt his own definition: "France was a land, England was a people, but America, having about it still that quality of the idea, was harder to utter – it was the graves at Shiloh and the tired, drawn faces of its great men, and the country boys dying in the Argonne for a phrase that was empty before their bodies withered. It was a willingness of the heart."

This wide-ranging philosophising might seem on the surface of things to take us a long way from the bootlegger Gatsby and his misconceived five-year passion for a girl who proves ultimately faithless. And yet perhaps it does not. Fitzgerald was not a man to forget a detail, certainly not one he had synthesised himself. His fictional Gatsby had himself served in the Argonne in 1918, and performed extraordinary heroics in command of his battalion's machine-guns, all to make himself worthy of the beloved object back home. Almost at the novel's outset its narrator, Nick Carraway, describes Gatsby's "extraordinary gift of hope, a romantic readiness such as I have never found in any other person..."

Yet, to insist on this link between such impulses and the country to which they are apparently unique in Fitzgerald's definition would, of course, make *The Great Gatsby* an inescapably American tale. Would it thereby diminish its significance? I think it would. Though we may admire the feelings that lead to the heartfelt verdict of a critic of Milton R. Stern's distinction: "The moving and lyrical prose in which the narrator's voice is finally a song of the significance of the author's life, indicates how completely and cohesively Fitzgerald had finally merged his vision, his memory and his materials into a moral history of the meaning of America" (*The Golden Moment*, 1970), we can't help feeling: "This isn't how art works!" Literature can never be corralled into delivering the moral history of a nation – at least, not without forfeiting its right to a place at the frontiers of imagination, as did the state-sponsored 'Socialist Realism' of the Soviet era in Russia. At Agincourt with King Henry V, Shakespeare is certainly not interested merely in the moral meaning of that particular historical confrontation. At the beginning of the play he has already amply demonstrated that the pretext for war against France is totally bogus. He is interested in courage and cowardice and the way men behave in the face of the unexpected.

Yes, Nick Carraway is the novel's narrator. But he is neither an omniscient voice nor a moral conduit. Indeed he is not even the sole narrator. We have sometimes to rely on him for an account of doings filtered by conversations he has had with other characters, sometimes Gatsby himself. Most important, he is also one of the novel's characters himself with, as we shall see, an autonomous individuality, and the frailties and prejudices that go with that. It is the distance that the use of Carraway in this dual role permits Fitzgerald to maintain between himself and his material that gives the book its extraordinarily lifelike quality. Far from being dragooned by a moral viewpoint, we are never entirely sure whose verdict on events we can completely trust, if anyone's, even the author's. The very epigraph to the book, the poem by Thomas Parke D'Invilliers, is a characteristic piece of Fitzgerald chicanery. The 'poet' of this name, who appears as a character in *This Side of Paradise*, turns out to be none other than Fitzgerald himself.

Finally, though *The Great Gatsby* is indisputably an American experience, certainly the most compelling portrait of the American 1920s – the Jazz Age – that we have, as Fitzgerald's masterpiece it demands to be judged alongside not just American, but world literature. If it is truly tragic, its tragedy must not be of a specifically American sort, but partaking of the universal tragic predicament.

2

Nick Carraway

As *The Great Gatsby*'s narrator, Nick Carraway places himself very precisely before us, both personally and geographically. His antecedents are solid but not spectacular. He is not a creature of excess, though that does not make him obtuse to its occurring in others. He is in many ways the *homme moyen sensuel*. What is important is that he is a mid-Westerner who has been bruised by his recent journey to the East which has become, for the purposes of this book and in a reversal of the American norm, the wild undiscovered frontier of human experience. "When I came back from the East last autumn, I felt that I wanted the world to be at a sort of moral attention for ever; I wanted no more riotous excursions with privileged glimpses into the human heart."

This sense of a comforting anchor in the geography, human and physical, of the Middle West is important throughout the novel and recurs towards its end in Nick's childhood memories of "the murky yellow cars of the Chicago, Milwaukee and St Paul railroad" and the "sprawling, swollen towns beyond the Ohio". At the opening of the book Nick's sensitivity to locality operates equally vividly as he considers the surrounds of his present domicile, at unfashionable West Egg on the shore of Long Island Sound, "the most domesticated body of salt water in the Western Hemisphere". As the days on the eastern seaboard grow hotter with the advance of summer Nick is to chronicle the feel of life on Long Island in extraordinary detail.

Unknown to him as he contemplates his eighty-dollars-a-month house, "squeezed between two huge places that rented for twelve or fifteen thousand a season," he has landed up alongside the story's eponymous protagonist. But Gatsby must wait. It is Nick's first social engagement, with a cousin,

Daisy and her husband, Tom, living in an adjacent part of Long Island, the more fashionable community of East Egg, that launches the action. Tom is, both physically and mentally, a brute and Nick, who had known him in college, is at no pains to disguise this. But Fitzgerald is far too skilful a creator to leave his character in the hands of Nick's prejudices. Daisy is interrupted in mid-sentence by her husband: " 'what are you doing Nick?' 'I'm a bond man.' 'Who with?' I told him. 'Never heard of them,' he remarked decisively."

We are immediately reminded of a character in a very different novel, Charles Wilcox in E. M. Forster's *Howard's End*. Both Forster and Fitzgerald are acutely alive to the crushing effect of the authoritarian character on those who come into contact with it. Tom does not wait for Nick's polite compliment on the very large house he is showing him around: 'I've got a nice place here ... It belonged to Demaine, the oil man.' Though it is not stated, we are left with the impression that Tom has stepped smartly in and profited from Demaine's misfortune. Tom exudes an intolerant power, and though it is a power based on inherited not created wealth, he exercises it confidently. When dinner is announced Nick observes with wry amusement: "Tom Buchanan compelled me from the room as though he were moving a checker to another square." With this same casual strength Buchanan will later smash his mistress' nose with a single blow to repay some perceived slight.

On any score of pure principle Nick would thoroughly disapprove of the women in Tom's ambit, Daisy and her friend Jordan Baker. At the end, in the wake of the double tragedy of Gatsby's and Myrtle's deaths, he is to dismiss Daisy in the same breath as Tom: "They were careless people, Tom and Daisy – they smashed up things and creatures and then retreated back into their money or their vast carelessness, or whatever it was that kept them together, and let other people clean up the mess they had made..."

But at this juncture – and this is one of the advantages of having the narrator as an autonomous character – as a man in the presence of young women, Nick is not at that "moral attention" his spirit later craves after the bruising it receives from events. His first sight of Daisy and her friend sitting on a couch in Tom's drawing room is a vision of two beautiful white birds "rippling and fluttering as if they had just been blown back in after a short flight round the house". If he is subsequently to suspect Daisy's honesty, he makes no attempt to play down her attractiveness now. "Her face was sad and lovely with bright things in it, bright eyes and a bright passionate mouth, but there was an excitement in her voice that men who had cared for her found it difficult to forget: a singing compulsion, a whispered 'Listen', a promise that she had done gay, exciting things just a while since and that there were gay, exciting things hovering in the next hour."

Our reactions to this are bound to be complex. Nick has furnished us with too potent a description of his cousin as a creature of fascination for us to set our minds against her on the score of the materialistic life choice she has made. We know that she is not simply a lovely inarticulate doll but a young woman of intelligence and wit, whose humorous sayings – and actions – are integral to the book. She preserves an ironical distance from the racist rant that bursts suddenly from Tom, based on some half-baked book, *The Rise of the Coloured Empires*, he has just read. 'Tom's getting very profound ... He reads deep books with long words in them.' (Interestingly, the terms of Tom's rant, which equates being 'Nordic' with man's achievements in 'civilisation – oh, science and art and all that' are no more outlandish than the sentiments Fitzgerald had himself expressed on Europe in a letter to Edmund Wilson from Paris in July 1921. "The negroid streak creeps northward to defile the Nordic race. Already the Italians have the souls of blackamoors. Raise the bars of immigration and permit only Scandinavians, Teutons, Anglo-Saxons and Celts to enter." It was an attitude of which he was to become ashamed enough on reflection to re-articulate it in the mouth of one of his most detestable characters.)

Jordan's appeal to Nick is far more direct. For one thing she is unattached. Nick tries his best not to like her. She takes no notice of him at first; she then speaks with contempt of the less fashionable part of Long Island in which he lives (somehow involving the name of Gatsby, whom she claims to have met, in that censure). To add to this Nick is subsequently to remember that he has heard something "unpleasant" about her. But he is on a hiding to nothing from the word go, as his rapid survey of her as a "slender, small-breasted girl" betrays. It is not that he is despising her for not being better endowed. Far from it: he is drawn to her with an attraction that is overwhelmingly sexual. Fitzgerald's great skill here is in not laying it on with a trowel.

As it happens Nick and Jordan are very shortly to be drawn into a conspiracy, even if it is only at first a conspiracy of shared information, that eventually brings them together as lovers. As dinner proceeds outside the house on the terrace the telephone rings within, abruptly injecting into the inconsequential indolence of the evening a dynamic of urgency. First the butler, then Tom and finally Daisy, too, go inside to attend to it leaving Nick alone with Jordan who reveals to him that Tom has 'some woman in New York'.

We are perhaps not that surprised. The 'golden girl' Daisy Fay for a wife, Demaine the oil man's house for a home, and a mistress to go with his marriage are, we imagine, pretty much par for the course for a man like Tom who has set no limits to the notion that he can possess anything he sees. Nick, by contrast, recoils with shock. If he was earlier in a fair way to succumbing to the enchantment that seemed to have possessed Daisy in her new, eastern, setting, he is suddenly censorious of her apparent acquiescence in the situation (" 'It couldn't be helped!' " cries Daisy "with tense gaiety" on her return to the table) without apparently asking himself whether she has any choice in the matter. In a tête-à-tête with her later that evening, he listens unmoved to her bitterness as she describes the circumstances of her daughter's birth: '...Tom was God knows where. I woke up out of the ether with

9

an utterly abandoned feeling, and asked the nurse right away whether it was a boy or a girl. She told me it was a girl and so I turned my head away and wept. "All right," I said, "I'm glad it's a girl. And I hope she'll be a fool – that's the best thing a girl can be in this world, a beautiful little fool." '

As he drives away at the end of the evening, "confused and a little disgusted," Nick reflects "It seemed to me that the thing for Daisy to do was to rush out of the house, child in arms – but apparently there were no such intentions in her head." No, there probably aren't. But is Nick being entirely realistic here? For better or for worse Daisy has married a provider, and if he turns out to be promiscuously unfaithful as well as a brute she is rather stuck with it. Women of the flapper generation may be allowed to be, as Daisy is, intelligent, witty, perceptive, fun-loving, the life and soul of the party. But their sexual liberation is a thing more apparent than real. And they are not, like the eponymous working-class heroine of Dreiser's *Sister Carrie*, creatures of great natural resource.

Earlier Nick had wondered whether "the whole evening had been a trick of some sort to exact a contributory emotion from me", and had concluded that Daisy's collusion in Tom's behaviour "asserted her membership in a rather distinguished secret society to which she and Tom belonged". It is beguilingly well put – Nick, while constantly proclaiming his ordinariness has a knack of putting things well. But I am not sure that the perception is sustainable from what follows. Would the Daisy Nick describes to us here have risked her membership of that club by re-igniting her affair with Gatsby as she does, even if she is found wanting at the final reckoning?

In all this ebb and flow of revelation and emotion the protagonist of the novel has all but been forgotten. His name was briefly mentioned at dinner by Jordan Baker, but it became submerged in the drama of the telephone call. We return to him at the end of the opening chapter. Arriving home with his thoughts in turmoil Nick sits out of doors for a while in a "loud, bright night, with wings beating in the trees". He suddenly becomes aware that Gatsby is out, too, standing on his adjacent lawn. He is on the verge of calling out to him when he realises that Gatsby is absorbed in a rapt manner in some object to seawards. "I could have sworn he was trembling. Involuntarily I glanced seaward – and distinguished nothing except a single green light, minute and far away, that might have been at the end of a dock."

The green light is to become one of the most powerful symbols in the book. Although he does not at that moment know it, Nick has caught his neighbour in that nightly moment of homage to the vision of Daisy that has sustained him over the past five years. After the disillusionment of Nick's evening it is Fitzgerald's genius to conceal the truth from his narrator. By the time he finally becomes aware of the magnitude of Gatsby's obsession, much more water has flowed under the bridge in respect of the dynamics of the Buchanan ménage, and Nick is in a frame of mind to be imaginatively alive to it.

3

The Waste Land

As a piece of scene setting Fitzgerald's creation of the valley of ashes set midway apparently between Nick's West Egg house and New York is both marvellous in itself and a most potent piece of symbolism. Overlooked by the spectacled eyes of Doctor T. J. Eckleburg, ("Evidently some wild wag of an oculist had set them there to fatten his practice in the borough of Queens...") it dominates the novel and remains in the mind as an object of fascination and horror long after the pages are closed on a first reading. The terrain of this part of Long Island compels the road and the railway to come together to cross "a small foul river, and when the drawbridge is up to let barges through, the passengers on waiting trains can stare at the dismal scene for as long as half an hour".

Consciously or not on Fitzgerald's part, there are inescapable parallels with the landscape, mental and physical, of parts of *The Waste Land*. T.S. Eliot's poem had been published in 1922, and we do not know to what degree Fitzgerald had absorbed its contents. But his valley immediately strikes us forcibly as a place "where the sun beats,/And the dead tree gives no shelter". From the measured ease of the lives of East Egg we descend here into a human culture which is somewhat analogous to that portrayed by Eliot in the second part of *A Game of Chess*, where urgent, vulgar, vernacular rhythms of speech take over from a remote survey of human prospects loftily cushioned by money. Over all this, the sightless eyes of Doctor Eckleburg, preside like those of the blind Tiresias of *The Fire Sermon* over an act of loveless coupling.

To enter the valley is to enter the land of the have-nots, and to savour, with the dust of the place in our mouths, the gulf that exists between them and the privileged residents of coastal Long Island. Two of its denizens are the proprietor of a dismal, run-down garage, George Wilson, and his wife Myrtle, whom Tom Buchanan has made his mistress. Wilson, seen through Nick's eyes, is a "blond, spiritless man, anaemic and faintly handsome". Tom patronises and bullies him with the promise of putting a little used-car business his way, while (barely bothering to conceal the fact behind Wilson's back) ordering his wife to take the train into New York at peremptorily short notice so that they can have sex in the apartment Tom has laid on there for the purpose. In contrast to her spiritless husband, we learn from Nick that "there was an immediately perceptible vitality about her as if the nerves of her body were continually smouldering".

We first encounter this ménage when Tom, enlivened by his lunchtime drinking at home, insists that Nick accompanies him to New York on the train, jumps off when it stops in the valley of ashes and drags him over to the garage 'to meet my girl'. On the apparently long-standing pretext that she is going to see her sister in New York, she travels up to town with them, discreetly distancing herself from them on the train. Tom is obviously not a mean lover in purely financial terms. Mrs Wilson makes free with his money without demur from him. As they take a cab from Pennsylvania Station to the apartment she stops impulsively to buy a puppy from a street vendor: 'for the apartment. They're nice to have – a dog.' We are not meant to like Myrtle, and Fitzgerald ensures that we don't. To the sheer vacuity of her desire in the purchase of the dog she adds a vulgarity that is always fighting with gentility. " 'Is it a boy or a girl?' she asked delicately. 'That dog? That dog's a boy' 'It's a bitch,' said Tom decisively. 'Here's your money. Go and buy ten more dogs with it.' "

Tom cuts through Myrtle's genteelism at the same time that he lets the wretched vendor know that he knows he is being fleeced, even when he does not want to demean himself by haggling in front of his woman. Nick, who does not want to be a party to this ghastly pair's unlovely adulterous coupling, desperately tries to cry off. But he is out of luck. So that he shan't feel like a wallflower, Mrs Wilson will telephone her sister who, we are apparently to assume, will not object to having sex with a stranger at short notice: 'She's said to be very beautiful by people who know.'

What follows is a brilliantly crafted chaotic and drink-fuelled social scene, as Myrtle, having apparently carte blanche from Tom to invite whom she likes to their love nest, sits on his knee while she calls up a host of guests for an impromptu party. Before any can arrive it is discovered that they are out of cigarettes and Nick is sent out to buy some from a street-corner drugstore. He arrives back to find that Tom and his "girl" have disappeared into a bedroom, "so I sat down discreetly in the living room and read a chapter of *Simon Called Peter* – either it was terrible stuff or the whisky distorted things because it didn't make any sense to me".

The topical reference is, appropriately, to the lurid novel of that title by Robert Keable (1887-1927) which had been published in 1921 and became a best-seller, largely owing to its controversial theme of the sexual temptation of an army chaplain serving in a French port during the First World War. It appears to be the only reading matter in Myrtle's apartment apart from *Town Tattle* and a clutch of scandal magazines.

Tom and Myrtle reappear from the bedroom, and guests begin to spill through the door, among them the sister "intended" for Nick, whom he observes as "a slender, worldly girl of about thirty with a solid sticky bob of red hair, and a complexion powdered milky white". The impression that she is probably a prostitute is reinforced when she laughingly tells Nick that she lives "with a girl friend at a hotel". Myrtle queens it magnificently over this gang of riff-raff. Tom does not, apparently, object to any of it, not even to her describing to the company their first encounter, which in her account becomes a grotesque parody of a lovers' meeting: 'When we came into the station he was next to me, and his white shirt

14

front pressed against my arm, and so I told him I'd have to call a policeman, but he knew I lied.' The detail of the policeman underlines the essential meretriciousness of it all.

Nick, meanwhile, with the exaggerated solicitude of the drunk, wipes from the slumbering face of one of the guests a spot of shaving foam that has been worrying him all afternoon and turns to observe that the poor puppy that has been purchased on such a reckless whim earlier in the day "was sitting on the table looking with blind eyes through the smoke, and from time to time groaning faintly". The hapless creature is the one true victim of this riot, none of whose other participants deserve much sympathy. The party and its guests occupy the lowest step on the social scale of such gatherings in *The Great Gatsby*. It is a claustrophobic indoor version of the grand (though no less chaotically inconsequential) soirées held by Gatsby, and has recognisable kinship with the New York "showdown" of Chapter VII.

Mrs Wilson seems to have got most things right in her assessment of what is due to her status as Tom's mistress. Essentially a vulgarian himself, he is not at all averse to sharing the trait with her. But with drink taking hold she oversteps the mark. She forgets that, like the East Egg house and like Daisy, she is merely a possession and a pretty lowly one on Tom's list at that. Tom may be a libertine but he is also a prig, and has a keen sense of what he regards as the sanctity of family life and the threat posed to it by the lax morality of the modern world.

When Myrtle makes light of Daisy's name, "Making a short, deft movement Tom broke her nose with his open hand." There is a nicely observed change of tempo, with "bloody towels upon the bathroom floor, and women's voices scolding". We leave the party with Tom's mistress weeping and bleeding copiously from her smashed face, trying vainly to preserve her precious tapestried couch from bloodstain damage with copies of *Town Tattle*.

It is another nice touch that on the way down in the lift the working man, abused at the outset of the scene in the person of the street vendor, gets his chance to fight back in a modest way against his 'betters', who are now in a state of some mental dishevelment. A guest is snapped at by the elevator boy when he drunkenly brushes the lever, and is forced to apologise with a fuddled attempt at dignity. The elevator boy has become, in his small way, symbolic of a state of order that the human party-goers have forfeited their right to inhabit through their behaviour. For Nick it is to be a long, cold hard-lying on a bench as he waits for the 4 a.m. train in the lower level of the Pennsylvania Station.

4

Ragtime at Trimalchio's

Trimalchio is the celebrated host of notoriously sumptuous Roman feasts in Petronius' comic fictional work of the 1st century AD, the *Satyricon*. Fitzgerald quite clearly sees his protagonist and his magnificent entertainments in terms of those of the Latin author. Nick is later to say of Gatsby when the pulse of his West Egg revels falls suddenly silent, "as obscurely as it had begun his carer as Trimalchio was over".

Indeed, among the many titles Fitzgerald considered as alternatives to *The Great Gatsby*, one was "Trimalchio in West Egg". We are thankful he did not finally choose it. But some of his other thoughts on naming the book were equally bad – most more so, viz "Gold-Hatted Gatsby", "The High-Bouncing Lover", "Among Ash-Heaps and Millionaires", "On the Road to West Egg", and a final, quite unsuitable, choice which, mystifyingly he most strenuously sought to impose on Scribner's at the last moment, "Under the Red, White and Blue". There are times when the 'creative' man needs firm guidance from his editors, and this was certainly one of them. Perkins told him that it was too late to change the plates.

Gatsby's version of Petronius' *Cena Trimalchionis* has the splendour of some exotic tropical kingdom about it. We might be thousands of miles – and years – away, in the court of Ravana the Demon King as he is first glimpsed by the questing Hanuman in the Sanskrit epic *Ramayana*. In the hot nights of the Long Island summer, the West Egg proceedings take on a dreamlike quality as Nick surveys them from afar. "In his blue gardens men and girls came and went like moths among the whisperings and the champagne and the stars." There is an air of evanescent, and undoubtedly somewhat febrile, enchantment.

Meanwhile tables groan under a freight of "glistening hors-d'oeuvre, spiced baked hams crowded against salads of harlequin designs and pastry pigs and turkeys bewitched to a dark gold". And among the crowds, "wanderers, confident girls who weave here and there" enjoy their "sharp, joyous moment" and then "glide on through a sea change of faces and voices". Fitzgerald is at the top of his descriptive power, here, and then: "Suddenly one of these gypsies, in trembling opal, seizes a cocktail out of the air, dumps it down for courage and, moving her hands like Frisco, dances out alone on the canvas platform. A momentary hush; the orchestra leader varies his rhythm obligingly for her, and there is a burst of chatter as the erroneous news goes round that she is Gilda Gray's understudy from the Follies. The party has begun."

The woman dancing on her own, having 'dumped down' a drink, is the defining touch. Suddenly the twentieth century has arrived, complete with its alcohol-dependent exhibitionist. If any description in the book encapsulates the Jazz Age, this does.

Most of these guests are gatecrashers, but on the occasion of his first visit to Gatsby's house Nick has actually been invited. "A chauffeur in a uniform of robin's-egg blue crossed my lawn early that morning with a surprisingly formal note from his employer." Whether or not this is Gatsby's standard modus operandi with strangers, it does in this instance establish a courtesy of dealings between the two men – so vastly differently circumstanced – that is to be preserved throughout the book. Although we have been living with the notion of Gatsby almost from page one, it comes as something of a surprise to us to realise that Nick does not actually meet him face to face until almost a third of the way through the book.

It is a party of tangential encounters of a mainly inconsequential sort. A variety of – mainly completely erroneous – opinions are passed on the host. He is variously a killer, a German spy, a wartime soldier, a man whose kind gesture in sending a young woman a replacement for a gown she has badly torn at one of his previous parties is deemed highly suspicious, not least by the friends of the (barely grateful) recipient of this generosity. Nick knows no one and finds it completely impossible to locate the host to introduce himself, since no one at the party seems either to know who Gatsby is, or to want to know. He is, he tells us, "on my way to get roaring drunk out of sheer embarrassment" (has he forgotten that he earlier in the book told us that he was only ever drunk twice in his life?), when Jordan appears. For Nick, Jordan and the sexual aura are indivisible. Her escort on the occasion is "a persistent undergraduate given to violent innuendo, and obviously under the impression that sooner or later Jordan was going to yield him up her person to a greater or lesser degree". We think she won't and that, in the fullness of time, it will be Nick to whom she turns. That is not for the moment important. What is, is that she knows both Gatsby and Daisy, and her increasing predilection for Nick is to draw him into the circle of that relationship.

En route to their eventual discovery of Gatsby, Nick and Jordan have what is apparently an inconsequential, circuitous conversation with a middle-aged man "with enormous owl-eyed spectacles" who is sitting in their host's library marvelling suddenly over the fact their host's books are "absolutely real – have pages and everything". We rather take to him, especially when he confesses: "I've been drunk for about a week now and I thought it might sober me up a bit to sit in a library." It is an intrinsically amusing episode, but also a pointedly symbolic one. Owl-eyes is clearly an incarnation of the ash valley's Doctor Eckleburg. Like T.S. Eliot's Tiresias, he will be there at the end of Gatsby's story, when everyone else save Nick and Gatsby's father have turned their backs on it.

Nick's introduction to Gatsby – they are at first for some time talking over wartime reminiscences without realising who each other is – is a highly ambivalent affair on Nick's side at least. Gatsby smilingly apologises for not making himself known as the host. "He smiled understandingly – much more than understandingly. It was one of those rare smiles with a quality of eternal reassurance in it." But just at the point that Nick is falling under the spell of Gatsby's apparently exquisite capacity for sensitivity to others, "it vanished – and I was looking at an elegant young rough-neck, a year or two over thirty, whose elaborate formality of speech just missed being absurd." This ambivalence on Nick's part is to receive an even severer test before the revelation that silences his scepticism.

At the end of the party, by which time "Most of the remaining women were now having fights with men said to be their husbands" and the blare of car horns reaches a crescendo as drunken drivers try to disentangle their vehicles from each other, Gatsby, a man on whom "no one swooned" and whose shoulder "no French bob touched" all evening is left in splendid isolation, bidding his guests goodnight, "his hand up in a formal gesture of farewell".

5

'Old Sport'

Notwithstanding the wilder claims that are made for his antecedents by several of the characters, not excluding Gatsby himself, and rather cleverly in a novel that is otherwise American to the core in its terms of reference, the litmus test of Gatsby's authenticity is made to become his claim to be "an Oxford man". It is a part of Fitzgerald's genius that he can make such a detail so symbolic a test of his protagonist's essential truthfulness, as Gatsby's background is progressively revealed and evidence (much more important) of his criminal associations comes to light.

The key, of course, to the power with which Fitzgerald can invest the symbol is in Nick's (and our) desire to believe in the man, and in the ebb and flow in the strength of that belief as the novel progresses. It is perhaps characteristic of this adroit manipulation of our feelings that, soon after Nick has met Gatsby, it is Jordan who is made to cast the first stone of doubt. 'I just don't think he went there,' she replies flatly to Nick's inquisition, and in spite of the fact that a young woman like Jordan would presumably be one of the least qualified of the characters to detect that particular imposture, we are inclined to believe her. An impostor herself (she has cheated at golf and lies to its owners about the damage she has caused to their car), she has, we may assume, the antennae to detect the quality in others. Nick does not want to believe her: "...young men didn't – at least in my limited provincial experience they didn't – drift coolly out of nowhere and buy a palace on Long Island Sound."

The question of proof surfaces again in a photograph of a college group Gatsby produces for Nick – which I think we are to understand as being in the category of the persuasive, rather than the absolutely conclusive. 'Proof' in *Gatsby* is always a provisional quality. The authenticity of Gatsby's claim is given no further impetus in the dubious testimony of the criminal Wolfshiem that his young associate has been "to Oggsford College in England ... one of the most famous colleges in the world". The huge gulf of ignorance this testimony demonstrates simply impugns the veracity of what is asserted.

And then, in the final showdown between Gatsby and Tom in New York, when so much is apparently at stake in terms of love and faith, and of who people really are, the detail surfaces again in a manner that makes it suddenly seem almost to be the most important piece of evidence for Gatsby's being worthy of Daisy. In the tense atmosphere of a stifling hotel room in the Manhattan August, with the sounds of a wedding party from the floor below acting as a mocking counterpoint to what is being enacted above, Tom appears at last to have Gatsby backpedalling on the claim. 'By the way, Mr Gatsby, I understand you're an Oxford man.' 'Not exactly.' 'Oh, yes, I understand you went to Oxford.' 'Yes – I went there.'

Tom, sure now of victory, pursues his man, "incredulous and insulting". It is worth quoting the passage in full to understand how Fitzgerald achieves such large psychological effects with apparently slight materials: "Another pause. A waiter knocked and came in with crushed mint and ice but the silence was unbroken by his 'thank you' and the soft closing of the door. This tremendous detail was to be cleared up at last. 'I told you I went there,' said Gatsby. 'I heard you, but I'd like to know when.' 'It was in nineteen-nineteen, I only stayed five months. That's why I can't really call myself an Oxford man.' Tom glanced round to see if we mirrored his unbelief. But we were all looking at Gatsby. 'It was an opportunity they gave to some of the officers after the armistice,' he continued. 'We could go to any of the universities in England or France.' I wanted to get up and slap him on the back. I had one of those complete renewals of faith in him that

I'd experienced before. Daisy rose, smiling faintly, and went to the table. 'Open the whisky, Tom,' she ordered. "

As we know, this is only to be round one in the contest. Yet Fitzgerald, with the establishment of the truth of "this tremendous detail" is able to imbue Gatsby's victory in this instance with a quality that seems far more important than his eventual defeat. He has, in fact, "turned out all right". Nick, whose faith, next to that of Gatsby, is the most important thing in the novel, is elated. Daisy, who, as we shall see later, is to be found completely wanting in what will follow, is at this juncture undeniably glad for her champion. She is so obviously 'on his side' at this moment that at the end it seems to me unjust, as much critical commentary does, to brand her entire dalliance with Gatsby as having been a cynical affair from the outset.

It has been a long hard road for Nick to arrive at this point of vindication for his belief. This is hardly surprising. Much earlier in the story, as the magnificent impression of his first visit to Gatsby's house recedes, the "person of some undefined consequence", whose lavish entertainments are constantly being punctuated by mysterious but apparently pressing long-distance business calls, has shrunk in the course of a series of pedestrian conversations with Nick to becoming "simply the proprietor of the elaborate roadhouse next door". Taken out by Gatsby for a lunch in New York, and regaled on the journey to a C.V. of manifestly improbable proportions – wealthy Middle West parents, now conveniently dead; living "like a young rajah in all the capitals of Europe"; big-game hunting; jewel collecting – Nick is conscious only of the absurdity of Gatsby's claims, wittily writing him down as "a turbaned 'character', leaking sawdust at every pore as he pursued a tiger through the Bois de Boulogne".

Most of the detail Gatsby imparts at this point is, indeed, as it will emerge, untrue. And why, when asked by Nick what part of the Middle West he comes from, does Gatsby reply 'San Francisco'? Are we to imagine that a man of any education whatsoever can be quite so ignorant of his country's geography, or is this Fitzgerald's way of indicating to us that though for the purposes of the novel its protagonists shall all be mid-Westerners, in spirit Gatsby does in fact belong to the West's remoter shores and is somehow linked with some Golden Gate of opportunity? Nick, and we the readers, are left to calculate a balance of probabilities in Gatsby's account of himself, which is not made any the easier by his next instalment: 'Then came the war, old sport…', surely another magnificent opportunity for rampant, unverifiable fantasy? Except that in this case the authentic enough sounding military exploits turn out to be true, and Gatsby can produce his decoration from 'little Montenegro down on the Adriatic Sea' for Nick's inspection.

Nick's education in the Gatsby ethos is to be completed over lunch, with the appearance at table of the mysterious and not a little sinister Meyer Wolfshiem. (This is the spelling of the name adopted by the UK Penguin edition, based on Fitzgerald's MS. For Scribner's second edition Edmund Wilson changed it to the more familiar Wolfsheim, and most critics have, either simply without noticing it or deliberately, made that adjustment in the spelling when writing about the character.) And who is this Wolfshiem? Nick asks. An actor? A dentist? " 'No, he's a gambler.' Gatsby hesitated, then added coolly: 'He's the man who fixed the World's Series back in 1919. ' "

The magnitude of the crime staggers Nick. 'Why isn't he in jail?' he splutters. 'They can't get him old sport. He's a smart man.'

Nick is by this time thoroughly in Gatsby's toils. The original purpose of his visit to New York had been a tea date with Jordan with whom he has begun to go around socially over the past few weeks. Though Nick likes to persuade himself that he feels "a sort of tender curiosity" for her, we are quite sure that the interest is entirely sexual. He is by now thoroughly acquainted with her dishonesty and has excused it: "Dishonesty in a woman is never a thing you blame deeply." In short, we can sense no kind of mental or emotional affinity that might subsist between the pair, and the attraction would seem to consist purely in her "cool, insolent smile" and his perception of her determination to "satisfy the demands of that hard, jaunty body". In the overall scheme of the depiction of sex in the book, this is as explicit as it ever gets.

Interestingly, Nick is at some pains to tell us at this juncture that he is "one of the few honest people I have ever known". This may well be true of his principled resolve to break it off with the girl he has back home before embarking on a serious siege of Jordan, but it does not apply to his approach to the new relationship. It is an interesting instance in the book of the narrator's completely parting company for a moment with the role that has been assigned him, with its burden of responsibility to the truth, and simply taking his place among the other characters.

But before lunch, Nick learns that his date with Jordan has already been hijacked by Gatsby. Jordan has been deputed 'to speak to you about this matter'. Annoyed at first, since "I hadn't asked Jordan to tea in order to discuss Mr Jay Gatsby", Nick nevertheless acquiesces, and in doing so gets back into role as the narrator of, from here on, irresistible events.

Jordan's story is soon told, and Nick is never quite the same man after it. Before America entered the war, in the summer of 1917, Daisy and Gatsby, a penniless young army lieutenant, had been in love. We take this as being far more than a matter of mere proximity on her part. She has to be restrained by her family from following him to New York to spend time with him before seeing him off overseas to France. By the time he returns from Europe in 1919 she is married to Tom. But before the wedding has actually taken place, a letter from Gatsby in France arrives at her house where she is being prepared as a bride. Jordan, who is one of her bridesmaids, enters her room to find her weeping and drunk on her bed, clutching a letter from Gatsby in her hand. She has flung the $350,000 pearl necklace Tom has given her into the waste basket. When Jordan comes in she fishes it out and tells her to return it to Tom. Thoroughly alarmed, Jordan nevertheless keeps her head and finds her mother's maid. Between them the women apply the cold bath, ice and ammonia treatment, and the day is saved. Daisy goes to her wedding next day dry-eyed. Tom's career of adultery has begun within weeks of the end of their South Seas honeymoon.

Still not fully understanding, Nick remarks on the coincidence of Daisy's and Gatsby's present proximity. Jordan tells him that it is no coincidence: 'Gatsby bought that house so that Daisy would be just across the bay.'

Suddenly the fabulous parties and the green light across the bay are explained. Nick's sympathies are from that moment engaged inescapably by the heroic passion to which his eyes have been opened. "Then it had not been merely the stars to which he had aspired on that June night. He came alive to me, delivered suddenly from the womb of his purposeless splendour." And when Jordan tells him that Gatsby merely wants him to ask Daisy to his house, so that Gatsby may 'drop by' and meet her, his reaction is: "The modesty of the demand shook me. He had waited five years and bought a mansion where he dispensed starlight to casual moths – so that he could 'come over' some afternoon to a stranger's garden."

Almost incidentally to these revelations, which are being concluded during a drive in a horse-drawn carriage in Central Park, Nick is, as it happens, to 'get' his girl, too. "It was dark now, and as we dipped under a little bridge I put my arm round Jordan's golden shoulder...". Unlike the Gatsby-Daisy conjunction this does seem very much a matter of night and opportunity. At the very point it happens we lose most of our, never very strong, interest in it. It never seriously challenges the imaginative thrall in which Nick is to be, from that point onwards, to Gatsby's love affair. It gives Nick something to do in the story, and gets him off stage when it suits Fitzgerald's purposes – that is about all.

6

Consummation

The moment has arrived at which Gatsby's modest proposal is to be put into execution. It is one of almost unbearable tension as five years of weighty expectation are to be subjected to the test of reality. Fitzgerald cleverly delays the confrontation, at the same time intensifying the sense of impending drama by a host of comic devices which serve a function not unlike that of the Porter scene in Shakespeare's *Macbeth*. They are an escape valve for our tightly wound emotions.

Gatsby, the effortless co-ordinator of magnificent entertainments suddenly becomes a domestic fusspot. Nick's dishevelled lawn is found wanting and must be trimmed by Gatsby's man. Nick's attempt at a few flowers to beautify his modest residence, to be purchased by his Finnish help from nearby West Egg village, are rendered nugatory by Gatsby's splendid provision: "at two o'clock a greenhouse arrived from Gatsby's with innumerable receptacles to contain it."

Does Daisy know what is afoot? Nick has been told by Jordan that she has made a point of asking her about the Gatsby whose name came up at the dinner party, and concluded "in the strangest voice that it must be the man she used to know". When Nick had invited Daisy for this tea engagement the day before with the rider not to bring Tom, her answer was 'Who is "Tom"?' When Daisy arrives, the "exhilarating ripple of her voice ... a wild tonic in the rain," she sustains the light-hearted mood: 'Are you in love with me ... or why did I have to come alone?', while we are all too aware that Gatsby, grey faced with tension is lurking outside, waiting to make his 'spontaneous' entry.

When he does, ridiculously soon after Daisy's arrival, we are treated to several pages of excruciating formality and awkwardness, as the protagonists in this tryst desperately try to imbue it with the significance of their collective memory. The agonising gaucheness of the process is beautifully observed by Nick. " 'We haven't met for many years,' said Daisy, her voice as matter-of-fact as it could ever be. 'Five years next November.' The automatic quality of Gatsby's answer set us all back at least another minute. "

With disaster apparently staring the whole project in the face, Nick can take no more and flees into the garden. When he returns he realises that some fundamental change has taken place. Although Nick announces his return through the kitchen in the noisiest possible way, "short of pushing over the stove", neither hears him come in. It is immediately apparent to him that something has 'happened'. Daisy's face is covered in tears, a fact we are at liberty to impute to regret for what is past and joy in the now – or a simple release of pent-up emotion. "But there was a change in Gatsby that was simply confounding. He literally glowed; without a word or gesture of exultation a new well-being radiated from him and filled the little room. "

From now on the afternoon is to be plain sailing. Or is it? Are we to be sceptical about whether each of the reunited lovers is actually sailing the same boat? The childish pleasure with which Gatsby suddenly wants to show Daisy round his house and possessions is absolved by Nick's commentary from being simply a display of competitive materialism: "I think he revalued everything in his house according to the measure of response it drew from her well-loved eyes." Nick paints for us a portrait of a man in the grip of sheer joy. "Once he nearly toppled down a flight of stairs" is a totally convincing detail and makes the man the more adorable in its sheer absurdity.

What are we to make of the episode of the shirts? It is a curious one. It seems too simplistic, in view of what has gone before, to say that Gatsby is wooing her with his material possessions, and that her reaction is simply an acquiescence in that. She can hardly be making comparisons. Tom can presumably afford just as many expensive shirts. In her paroxysm of weeping she actually says something rather different. 'It makes me sad because I've never seen such – such beautiful shirts before.' The point made is that, notwithstanding the vulgarity of the trappings with which he woos the world, Gatsby is capable of beauty. As for Gatsby's introducing the shirts in the first place, it is rather in the category of his nearly falling down the stairs, as he did earlier, than being a piece of simple ostentation. As Nick acutely observes, by this stage of the afternoon Gatsby is beginning to enter on a state of emotional exhaustion. "He had been full of the idea [of Daisy's presence] so long, dreamed it right through to the end, waited with his teeth set, so to speak, at an inconceivable pitch of intensity. Now, in the reaction, he was running down like an over-wound clock." In such a condition a man may do many absurd things – including showing off his shirts.

The chapter is vitally important not just for the obvious reason that in it we see the two former lovers reunited, but because it is the only one in which we see them at close quarters together. Of course Nick is in the frame, too, but from the moment the understanding between them is achieved, his presence is purely as a narrator. In the two subsequent chapters, Gatsby's second party and the New York showdown, Tom's forceful, simplistic personality dominates.

We know what Gatsby stands for in the relationship, but Daisy has had a pretty bad press from the critics. Is she, as the object of Gatsby's quest, simply a figment of his imagination, but in reality "a treacherous whore" (Martin Seymour-Smith, *New Guide to Modern World Literature*, 1985) or, as Rena Sanderson puts it ("Women in Fitzgerald's Fiction", *Cambridge Companion to F. Scott Fitzgerald*, 2002), occupying "a prominent place in the American literary tradition that features females of questionable morality"? Whatever the answer to the question is, it need not at all detract from the magnificence of Gatsby's colossal dream. And yet that dream gains considerably from the idea that he has not in the first instance fallen in love with a mirage.

As we saw earlier, Nick only turns definitively on Daisy at the end, by which time his love affair with the East is over and he has recovered much of his sturdy Middle Western moral conservatism. But in this chapter we receive no hint from him that she is beyond the pale of Gatsby's regard. That regard, and the sheer hugeness of what it sets itself, carry within them, as he makes clear, the inevitable seeds of their own disillusionment. When Gatsby confesses to her that the green light at the end of her dock has always been a talisman, she impulsively puts her arm through his. But in that very instance, as Nick observes: "... he seemed absorbed in what he had just said. Possibly it had occurred to him that the significance of that light had now vanished forever ... It had seemed as close as a star to the moon. Now it was again a green light on a dock. His count of enchanted objects had diminished by one."

We are at liberty to reject this as being a trifle too fanciful in terms of what we know of the way Gatsby's mind sees things. It is perhaps an over-refinement of disillusionment, a perception that Nick's more sceptical mentality (in affairs of the heart at least) has saddled Gatsby with. There is greater truth, it seems to me, in his reflection on Gatsby as he goes to take his leave of the lovers, who are by this time totally absorbed in each other. "There must have been moments even that afternoon when Daisy tumbled short of his dreams – not through her own fault, but because of the colossal vitality of his illusion." And yet, the quality of this rekindled love has, in this scene, the last word. "I looked once more at them and they looked back at me, remotely, possessed by intense life. Then I went out of the room and down the marble steps into the rain, leaving them there together." This powerfully expressed vision of love, which includes Daisy as surely as it does Gatsby, carries simply too much conviction for it to be open to Nick to take it back dismissively at a later date.

We are not to see Gatsby or Daisy in possession of such happiness again in the novel. There is almost immediately, at the outset of the next chapter, a sense that the world is closing in on the protagonist. A New York reporter has "heard Gatsby's name around his office in a connection he either wouldn't reveal or wouldn't understand", and turns up on his doorstep to ask him if he has anything to say.

" 'Anything to say about what?' inquired Gatsby politely." But a certain amount of mud has stuck, about shady business dealings, "spread about by the hundreds who had accepted his hospitality and so become authorities upon his past".

A planned novel requires carpentry, and we are perhaps for the first and only time aware of its obtruding here. The narrator of this episode is scarcely to be identified with Nick, who by his own admission is not in touch with Gatsby and does not see him for several weeks, taken up as he is with his affair with Jordan Baker. Fitzgerald seems momentarily to have taken over as his deputy. It does not much matter. It is an opportunity for us to get some more apparently authentic background on the manner in which James Gatz of North Dakota, the son of "shiftless and unsuccessful farm people" becomes Jay Gatsby of West Egg via his career as "steward, mate, skipper, secretary and even jailor" to the self-made millionaire Dan Cody, whose yacht he has saved from destruction from the wind in a treacherous anchorage over a shallow flat on Lake Superior. The very name Cody here carries a symbolic charge in terms of its firm association with American "can do" endeavour. The fictional Dan Cody is irresistibly linked in our minds with the famous frontiersman and entrepreneur William "Buffalo Bill" Cody and the pioneer American aviator Samuel Cody (who among other things was to build the first British military aircraft).

"He [Gatsby] told me all this very much later," Nick tells us, and we are relieved when he comes back to us out of the arms of Jordan, and positions himself again in the centre of the story.

The tempo of the novel picks up again when Nick becomes a witness to a chance meeting between Gatsby and Tom Buchanan, the latter dropping in at the West Egg house, while out riding with some acquaintances who also happen to know

Gatsby. Tom is of course totally unaware of what has transpired between his wife and Gatsby, of whom he has barely heard. We instinctively fear for Gatsby who is clearly not under complete control of himself in this proximity to a hated rival whom he considers himself to have vanquished. His conviction of being secure of Daisy's love leads to his aggressively insisting on his acquaintanceship with Tom's wife in a manner that serves only to put Buchanan on his guard. The libertine immediately turns guardian of home and hearth: 'I wonder where the devil he met Daisy. By God, I may be old fashioned in my ideas, but women run around too much these days to suit me.' As a result he insists on accompanying her to Gatsby's next party, a circumstance which, as Nick records, "gave the evening its peculiar quality of oppressiveness".

Unaware of all this Daisy, however, is in skittish mood, happy to use Nick theatrically as a sort of surrogate for her love for Gatsby that can't be articulated. " 'These things excite me *so*,' she whispered. 'If you want to kiss me any time during the evening, Nick, just let me know and I'll be glad to arrange it for you. Just mention my name. Or present a green card. I'm giving out green –' "

Daisy and Gatsby dance, and he – as we are – is "surprised by his graceful conservative foxtrot". It is to be her only passage of true pleasure in an evening of fractiousness. When, shortly afterwards, she watches a movie director lean over and place a reverential kiss on his young star's cheek after a long, slow coming together that has been going on all evening, she immediately transfers the significance of it to herself and her own happiness: " 'I like her,' said Daisy, 'I think she's lovely.' " It is a beautifully wrought moment in which Daisy's apparently totally mundane, not to say naive, observation is made to speak volumes.

But it seems to me that here again Nick goes on to cloud the truth of his perceptions by over-analysis. "But the rest offended her ... She was appalled by West Egg, this unprecedented 'place' that Broadway had begotten upon a Long Island fishing village

– appalled by the raw vigour that chafed under the old euphemisms ... She saw something awful in the very simplicity she failed to understand." Such a viewpoint is far too complicated (and in the end far too muddled) to be Daisy's. She is good at the direct things, and Nick is at his best when he is recording without comment, as he does sitting with Tom and Daisy as they wait for their car at the end of the evening. Tom breaks brutally in on the reflective silence with the accusation that 'to get this menagerie together' Gatsby must be a bootlegger or something similarly crooked. " 'At least they are more interesting than the people we know,' she said with an effort."

Tom will not let it lie, but she refuses to be further drawn. Instead, she "began to sing with the music in a husky, rhythmic whisper ... and each change tipped out a little of her warm, human magic." Tom's intervention with all its worldly innuendo is powerless to shake her conviction. We are to understand, it seems to me, that her love for Gatsby has enabled her to slough off the veneer of cynical artificiality that has been essential to her mental survival in her marriage to Tom. Under its influence she has been able to find a way back to becoming that more authentic individual who was able, under the influence of Gatsby's letter, to throw Tom's pearl necklace in her wastebasket. As we shall see, she never makes it.

7

Showdown

In the tragic denouement Gatsby is, of course, his own worst enemy. As Nick, now clear-sighted, observes regretfully, "He wanted nothing less of Daisy than that she should go to Tom and say: 'I never loved you.' " And when Nick counsels him that insisting on this will be to ask too much of her and that one cannot repeat the past in so literal a manner, Gatsby is obstinately incredulous. 'Why, off course you can!'

By the time the crux confrontation scene opens Gatsby's career as Trimalchio is over. Are we to be surprised at that? He has 'got' the girl and does not need to give parties in the hope that she will arrive one evening, like the others, as an uninvited guest. A new, discreet regime has taken over the running of what has been open house at West Egg. Nick's gloss on it is that "the whole caravansary had fallen in like a card house at the disapproval in her eyes". Disapproval of what?

Gatsby has just told him that it is a matter of discretion. 'Daisy comes over quite often – in the afternoons.' Gatsby, as Wolfshiem earlier told Nick, 'would never so much as look at a friend's wife'. (A crook in business, Wolfshiem need not be distrusted in his sense of domestic propriety.) And in his own strange way Gatsby has adhered to the code of conduct attributed to him. He had earlier turned down in indignation Jordan's suggestion that he make his first play for Daisy by asking her out to lunch in New York as being a move that would compromise her as a married woman. He wants Daisy first publicly to disown her marriage so that he can possess her 'legitimately' in the eyes of the world.

He now calls Nick to tell him that Daisy has invited them both (and Jordan) to lunch at the Buchanan house. Nick is worried – and so are we. "Something was up. And yet I couldn't believe that they would choose this occasion for a scene."

The scene that confronts Nick's entry to the house designedly bears an eerie similarity in so many details to that of his first visit in the opening chapter. It is again a hot day. Daisy and Jordan, clad in white dresses, as we first saw them, are lying immovable on an enormous couch. Tom is on the phone, summoned this time not as Jordan provocatively asserts, by his 'girl', but, as it would appear, by her husband Wilson about a car he has promised to sell to him.

We can see by now what a potent symbol the phone, that modern (in 1925) means of communication by which powerful men like Tom and Gatsby can make their decisions without having to come face to face with their interlocutors, has been throughout the novel. It was the instrument through which we first learnt that the glossy surface life of Nick and Daisy was not what it appeared to be. It is the means through which the unreal pantomime of Gatsby's parties is constantly punctuated with the suggestion of untoward doings behind the scenes. Even in the midst of the happy wooing of Daisy by Gatsby, it intrudes again, creating a sense of unease as we are made party to the strange, ill-tempered sentence from Gatsby to someone else at the end of the line: 'Well, he's no use to us if Detroit is his idea of a small town …'.

Here, with Wilson evidently pleading for a favour, it returns us to the abyss of misery, where human problems are exacerbated by the careless cruelty of men like Tom. The link to the waste land of ashes is thus cleverly re-established by Fitzgerald. Though we are not to know it at this juncture, it is where the end of Gatsby's journey will begin.

The difference from the opening scene of course is the presence of Gatsby. He has so far said nothing. We are conscious of his simply standing in the centre of the crimson carpet and taking in surroundings about which we know he must have a painfully intense curiosity, so completely is he in denial of there ever having been any valid meaning in Daisy's and Tom's life together. When he is greeted by Tom, after the latter concludes his telephone call and joins them, it is with "well concealed dislike". Daisy immediately orders her husband out of the room to make them all a drink, and the formalised inertia of the scene is given an unexpected jolt. "As he left the room again she got up and went over to Gatsby and pulled his face down, kissing him on the mouth. 'You know I love you,' she murmured."

The naked eroticism of this simple gesture makes for a surprisingly potent moment. All the other kisses imagined or described between Gatsby and Daisy in the book have been sketched in somewhat ethereal terms, or imbued with a freight of somewhat distant metaphysical significance that they can hardly support. This is refreshingly 'rude'. It is also exhilaratingly dangerous with Tom so close at hand. Daisy is in a determined mood as far as her love is concerned. When rebuked as a 'vulgar girl' by Jordan, she replies 'I don't care!' and begins "to clog on the brick fireplace", the jazz girl in defiant rebellion against the cold convention of her marriage.

In spite of the potentially explosive emotional components working here, lunch is somehow negotiated and, again in a brilliant echo of the opening chapter, in which Tom offered to take Nick to the stables, he is actually prosing away to Gatsby about how clever he is to have been able to adapt a garage for stabling purposes, when Daisy cuts across him. "Gatsby's eyes floated towards her. 'Ah,' she cried, 'you look so cool.' Their eyes met and they stared together at each other, alone in space … She had told him that she loved him, and Tom Buchanan saw."

In the first part of the book we moved from East Egg, via the valley of ashes to a claustrophobic New York party which became chaotic under the weight of alcohol. Now in a skilfully devised run-up to the novel's denouement, we almost precisely reprise this progress. The party will ride in two cars, Tom's coupé and Gatsby's big yellow contraption, which, at his insistence, Tom will drive – if only to prove a point to Gatsby. He has gained a small and apparently pointless victory over Gatsby. (It is only later that we shall see its significance.) Yet in the object he really wants to achieve Tom for once fails to get his way. Desperate to reassert his control over Daisy, he demands that she travel with him. She eludes his encircling arm and "walked close to Gatsby, touching his coat with her hand". It is they who end up driving to town together.

Tom, Nick and Jordan arrive under the eyes of Doctor Eckleburg at Wilson's garage where Gatsby's car is in need of petrol. By now the whole edifice of Tom's life is beginning to crumble. Wilson, like Tom, has realised that his wife has 'another life', and tells him that they are getting away to the West. Tom's reaction is nicely observed by Nick: "... as we drove away Tom was feeling the hot whips of panic. His wife and mistress, until an hour ago so secure and inviolate were slipping precipitately from his control."

In what is the most crowded, tautly plotted chapter in the novel, Fitzgerald has, while negotiations for petrol are still in progress on the garage forecourt, been able to insert, in a few sentences, a detail whose importance is likely to pass us by at the time; but it is to become the trigger for the subsequent tragedy of three deaths. As Daisy does not know who her love rival is, Myrtle likewise has no idea what Tom's wife looks like. As Tom talks to Wilson, Nick realises that the giant eyes of Doctor Eckleburg are not the only ones keeping a vigil. From her room over the garage, Myrtle Wilson is peering down at the car, and, Nick supposes at first, at Tom her lover, "until I realised that her eyes, wide with jealous terror, were fixed not on Tom, but on Jordan Baker, whom she took to be his wife". The authorial device of the car switch for the outward journey will become apparent when on the return journey, the conspicuous yellow automobile, this time with the real Mrs Buchanan at the wheel, will encounter the hapless Mrs Wilson on its return journey from New York.

In New York, after aimlessly drifting around trying to find something worthwhile to do, to pass the time, we end up in a stifling room of the Plaza Hotel where "opening the windows admitted only a gust of hot shrubbery from the Park". It is here, as we saw in chapter 5, that Gatsby triumphantly survives round one of his confrontation with Tom.

It is not enough. Unfortunately for Gatsby, Tom has not the imagination to know when he has been bested. When he directly challenges Gatsby with 'causing a row in my house' we sense that for the first time, instead of having eyes for Gatsby only, Daisy is "looking desperately from one to the other". The psychological dynamics of the encounter are nicely observed. At first Daisy puts up stout resistance to Tom's hypocrisy. 'Once in a while I go off on a spree and make a fool of myself, but I always come back, and in my heart I love her all the time.'

" 'You're revolting,' said Daisy. She turned to me, and her voice, dropping an octave lower, filled the room with thrilling scorn." Yet it is her last real throw as the balance of power gradually shifts decisively back towards Tom. Gatsby simply has not thought clearly about the tactics that might have brought him victory. He cannot offer Daisy the kind of support she needs at this pinch. His childish insistence on hearing her say the words he wants uttered, 'I never loved him', is just too much for her. As she tries to explain to him, that much simply cannot be true. " 'Oh you want too much!' she cried to Gatsby. 'I love you now – isn't that enough? I can't help what's past.' She began to sob helplessly. 'I did love him once – but I loved you too.' "

To hear that he has been loved 'too' is the body blow for Gatsby. From then on he is in retreat. Having previously defended him against charges of bootlegging, Daisy must now listen while Tom details what sounds like conclusive proof of the criminal basis of Gatsby's wealth. It is all over. Tom is able "with magnanimous scorn" to tell her to go home – this time in Gatsby's car. " 'Go on. He won't annoy you. I think he realises that his presumptuous little flirtation is over.' They were gone, without a word, snapped out, made accidental, isolated, like ghosts, even from our pity."

On the return journey Gatsby unwisely allows Daisy, by this time a nervous wreck, to take the wheel. As they pass by the Wilson garage, Myrtle, seeing the yellow car, comes out presumably with some idea of accosting Tom, whom she takes to be its owner. Daisy swerves to avoid her, then swerves back, over-compensating in her fright at the approach of an oncoming car. She hits Myrtle, who is killed. Gatsby takes her back to East Egg, and agrees to shoulder the blame. In the event he is not to live long enough to be required to do that. In subsequent conversations with Wilson, Tom will make sure that the bereaved and now deranged garage owner knows fully who the 'guilty' owner of the yellow car is, and where he lives.

Meeting Nick later, surreptitiously outside the Buchanans' house, Gatsby still clings pathetically to hope. " 'She'll be all right tomorrow,' he said presently. 'I'm just going to wait here and see if he tries to bother her about that unpleasantness this afternoon. She's locked herself into her room, and if he tries any brutality she's going to turn the light out and on again.' " We would like to believe this nonsense but in reality we are as sick at heart as Nick is about the outcome. Gatsby has not yet recognised the utter defeat of his grand design and the collapse of his vision. Sneaking round the back of the house in an attempt to check on the pair, Nick is soon to receive proof of it. Through a gap in a blind he sees them "sitting opposite each other at the kitchen table ... He was talking earnestly across the table at her, and in his earnestness his hand had fallen upon and covered her own ... There was an unmistakable air of natural intimacy about the picture".

Reporting back to Gatsby as he has promised, Nick has not the heart to tell him of his findings, and leaves him "standing there in the moonlight – watching over nothing".

8

Reckoning

There is still more to come from Gatsby before his violent death at the hands of the deranged Wilson. And we are constantly, even in what we know to be the waning moments of his life, astonished at the intensity which with he preserves the image of Daisy. There is something almost unendurably touching in the tenacity of his memories as he relates them to Nick. 'I can't describe to you how surprised I was to find out I loved her, old sport.' The very refrain 'old sport', which struck us when we first heard it as an affectation, has now taken on a quality of all-embracing tenderness. We might almost fancy that as Wilson aimed the gun at him Gatsby would have said understandingly: 'That's all right, old sport.'

Both men are assuredly Tom's victims. Is Daisy directly implicated in their deaths, too? Nick implies as much, though whether he means us to assume that she understands, and deliberately fails to warn Gatsby of, the threat from the approaching Wilson, is not absolutely clear. In any event his final verdict on her is a complete negation of the vision of her he gave us in the throes of her rekindled love for Gatsby.

Wilson dies in a state of bitter disillusionment. His grief over the loss of a supposed future to be lived with a wife we know to be faithless is one of the most powerfully handled episodes in the book. He, too, has briefly had his dream, and events that are not remotely his fault are cruelly to extinguish it.

Does Gatsby die with his vision of what has now become a fantasy intact, waiting in the splendid glow of his confidence for a telephone call from Daisy that we know will never come? Nick as narrator thinks not. "I have an idea that Gatsby himself didn't believe it would come, and perhaps he no longer cared. If that was true he must have felt that he had lost the old warm world, paid a high price for living too long with a single dream.'"

Yet at this very moment, when the pointlessness of it all is borne in on Nick with a force that will ultimately cause him to flee from the scene and find comforting refuge again in the familiar moral ethos of the Middle West, he is aware perhaps as never before of the splendour that is Gatsby. 'You're worth the whole damn bunch together' is his shouted farewell as he leaves him for the last time. And Gatsby dead continues to speak to Nick with the vividness of Gatsby alive. 'Look here, old sport, you've got to get somebody for me. You've got to try hard. I can't go through this alone.' As all Gatsby's business associates sheer off in alarm, assuming that the killing has a gangster dimension to it, Nick begins to develop "a feeling of defiance, of scornful solidarity between Gatsby and me against them all".

Having had some patchy moments in terms of his perception of events, Nick now appears as a more sympathetic individual than at any time in the novel. We like the fruitless effort he puts in to persuading such associates as Wolfshiem and Klipspringer to come to Gatsby's funeral. It is a particularly nice touch that the latter has phoned not to find out about the funeral but to ask if a pair of shoes he has left at the West Egg house can be sent on to him. " 'My address is care of B. F. –' I didn't hear the rest of the name because I hung up the receiver." In receiving such an education in the hardness of the human heart, Nick is at last finding some steel in the depths of his own nature.

The cemetery interment "in a thick drizzle" and the hearse "horribly black and wet" is acted out in that ambience of atmospheric pathetic fallacy to which funerals are prone in literature. Apart from the necessary officiating clergyman, a few villagers and the pathetically proud father ('Jimmy was bound to get ahead'), the only other mourner, an appearance of great surprise to Nick, is Owl-eyes, struggling with his pebble glasses in the pouring rain to follow the details of the interment. His startlingly loud 'Amen to that' in response to a murmured beatitude whose source we are deliberately kept ignorant of, seems symbolically to draw a line under Gatsby's career. His more demotic 'poor son of a bitch' in wondering response to Nick's informing him that no others but those he now sees have been at the funeral service, is Tiresias' final commentary on the bathos of the proceedings.

Yet, in all Nick's disillusionment at the end of the book, embracing as it does Jordan, whom he rejects, as well as Tom, Daisy and the thanklessness of those who have taken Gatsby's hospitality and then spurned him, Gatsby himself burns as steadfastly before him as Daisy's green light did to Gatsby, sustaining his share of the dream. We can I suppose take or leave the symbolism of the moment when Nick, taking his final leave of West Egg, finds a cleansing inspiration in locating the origins of Gatsby's dream in the wonder that the first Dutch sailors felt when they set eyes on Long Island, and the "fresh, green breast of the new world". This particular geographical location of the purity of human impulses is more likely to appeal to Americans than Europeans.

It is heartfelt nevertheless. Amidst the tawdriness of all that preyed on him, Gatsby, as we learnt at the outset, "turned out all right in the end". We are content, with Nick at the end of the book, to see in the dream of Gatsby, the green light in which he believed, the "orgastic future" for which it stands, a vital, redeeming force towards which, no matter that it has eluded us today, "tomorrow we will run faster, stretch our arms further ... And one fine morning – " The life of Gatsby, in all its apparent futility and failure, has imbued Nick with a vision of the potential for hope dwelling in the human spirit. It is a vision that he would never have glimpsed had he not strayed off the ground of moral certainties nurtured by an upbringing in his native Middle West.

Further Reading

Critical and biographical studies

John B. Chambers: *The Novels of Scott Fitzgerald*
(Macmillan, 1989). Perceptive study which in the instance
of *Gatsby* makes an unexpected but persuasive comparison
of Fitzgerald's protagonist with that of E. M. Forster's
The Longest Journey.

K. G. W. Cross: *Scott Fitzgerald* (Oliver and Boyd, 1964).
A thoughtful account in this very useful, concise Writers
and Critics series, which is good on all the novels, and
particularly so on *Gatsby.*

Leslie A. Fiedler: *Love and Death in the American Novel*
(Criterion Books, 1960). Fitzgerald is of course one among
many authors surveyed here, but this provocative study is
essential background reading.

Andrew Hook: *F. Scott Fitzgerald: A Literary Life* (Palgrave
Macmillan, 2002).
Not exactly biography nor yet straight criticism, but an
interesting exploration of the creative processes behind
Fitzgerald's novels, with useful insights into his own
motivation and aspirations.

Edited by Arthur Mizener: *F. Scott Fitzgerald* (Prentice-Hall,
1963). Wide-ranging selection of essays, by some of the major
names of the period, on all Fitzgerald's works covering the
first 30-odd years of criticism in this excellent Twentieth
Century Views series. Good introduction by Mizener and
a particularly interesting essay on *Gatsby* by A. E. Dyson.

Edited by Ruth Prigozy: *The Cambridge Companion to F. Scott Fitzgerald* (Cambridge University Press, 2002). A collection of specially commissioned essays, giving a contemporary take on various aspects of issues raised by Fitzgerald's novels. Useful insights from an all-American team that includes Ronald Berman (on *Gatsby*), Rena Sanderson (on women in Fitzgerald's fiction), Milton R. Stern and Prigozy herself.

Milton R. Stern: *The Golden Moment: The Novels of F. Scott Fitzgerald* (University of Illinois Press, 1970). Although describing this modestly as "an old-fashioned and personal book", Stern provides a comprehensive survey of Fitzgerald's fiction, its genesis, context and interpretation, and his long chapter on *Gatsby* is remarkable in its insights.

GREENWICH EXCHANGE BOOKS

STUDENT GUIDE LITERARY SERIES

The Greenwich Exchange Student Guide Literary Series is a collection of essays on major or contemporary serious writers in English and selected European languages. The series is for the student, the teacher and 'common readers' and is an ideal resource for libraries. The *Times Educational Supplement* praised these books, saying, "The style of [this series] has a pressure of meaning behind it. Readers should learn from that ... If art is about selection, perception and taste, then this is it."

(ISBN prefix 978-1-871551 applies unless marked*, when the prefix 978-1-906075 applies.)

The series includes:
Antonin Artaud by Lee Jamieson (98-3)
W.H. Auden by Stephen Wade (36-5)
Honoré de Balzac by Wendy Mercer (48-8)
William Blake by Peter Davies (27-3)
The Brontës by Peter Davies (24-2)
Robert Browning by John Lucas (59-4)
Lord Byron by Andrew Keanie (83-9)
Samuel Taylor Coleridge by Andrew Keanie (64-8)
Joseph Conrad by Martin Seymour-Smith (18-1)
William Cowper by Michael Thorn (25-9)
Charles Dickens by Robert Giddings (26-9)
Emily Dickinson by Marnie Pomeroy (68-6)
John Donne by Sean Haldane (23-5)
Ford Madox Ford by Anthony Fowles (63-1)
The Stagecraft of Brian Friel by David Grant (74-7)
Robert Frost by Warren Hope (70-9)
Patrick Hamilton by John Harding (99-0)
Thomas Hardy by Sean Haldane (33-4)
Seamus Heaney by Warren Hope (37-2)
Joseph Heller by Anthony Fowles (84-6)
Gerard Manley Hopkins by Sean Sheehan (77-3)
James Joyce by Michael Murphy (73-0)
Philip Larkin by Warren Hope (35-8)
Laughter in the Dark – The Plays of Joe Orton by Arthur Burke (56-3)
George Orwell by Warren Hope (42-6)